Th___ ___ ___
Addiction

....

How God Redeems Our Pain

Erik Guzman

New
Growth
Press

newgrowthpress.com

New Growth Press, Greensboro, NC 27404
newgrowthpress.com

Cover Design: Tandem Creative, Tom Temple,
   tandemcreative.net
Typesetting: Lisa Parnell, lparnell.com

ISBN: 978-1-942572-85-5 (Print)
ISBN: 978-1-942572-86-2 (eBook)

Library of Congress Cataloging-in-Publication Data
   Names: Guzman, Erik, 1972– author.
   Title: The gift of addiction : how God redeems our pain / Erik
Guzman.
   Description: Greensboro, NC : New Growth Press, 2016.
   Identifiers: LCCN 2015040565 | ISBN 9781942572855
(pbk.) | ISBN 9781942572862 (ebook)
   Subjects: LCSH: Addicts—Religious life. | Substance
abuse—Religious aspects—Christianity.
   Classification: LCC BV4596.A24 G89 2016 | DDC
248.8/629—dc23
   LC record available at http://lccn.loc.gov/2015040565

Printed in India

28 27 26 25 24 23 22 21   3 4 5 6 7

So, you did it again, didn't you? You promised you wouldn't, but you did.

What was it? Did you wake up still drunk, wondering how you got home? Was it gambling? Was it another night alone with the computer? Maybe you weren't alone—maybe you were with him or her again? Food? Drugs? Was it rage at someone who dared to question your perfectly constructed religious system?

Is another promise to change really going to turn out any different? Look where all your promises got you. You're too ashamed to get help. And God . . . well, you prayed, you made commitments, and you even begged him to take away your thorn in the flesh, but that obviously hasn't made much difference.

What would you say if I told you that your addiction is actually a gift from God? What if it's actually the key to your transformation? Well, it's true. God can use your addiction to make you more compassionate, creative, and connected while, at the same time, ensuring that your compulsions begin to lose their control of your life. You really can live sober.

Living Sober

"We admitted we were powerless over alcohol—that our lives had become unmanageable." That's the first of the Twelve Steps of Alcoholics Anonymous. Given that you've picked up this little book, you might be ready to admit that you're powerless over your addiction. At the very least you're probably thinking you have a problem. Admitting you have a problem may be the first step in solving it, but if you don't correctly identify the problem, trying to fix it will just make it worse.

That's why it's so important to realize that your addiction isn't your biggest problem. Sure, it causes problems, but it's not *the* problem. The real problem is that we are creatures made for union with God who are suffering in self-imposed isolation.

In case that just sounds like religious jargon, here's what the psychiatrist Carl Jung famously wrote in a letter about an alcoholic patient of his:

> His craving for alcohol was the equivalent, on a low level, of the spiritual thirst of our being for wholeness, expressed in medieval language: the union with God . . . You see, "alcohol" in Latin is *spiritus* and you use the same word for the highest religious experience as well as for the most depraving poison. The helpful formula therefore is: *spiritus contra spiritum.*[1]

Spiritus contra spiritum means "spirituality against spirits." This concept is the seed that ultimately grew into Alcoholics Anonymous. The Twelve Steps actually guide the addict toward spiritual awakening. That's because living sober is way more than putting down the bottle. Any drunk will tell you that being dry is not the same as being sober.

The need for sobriety is universal. To live sober strikes at the heart of what it means to be fully human. To put it succinctly, living sober means embracing reality.

Sobriety is not simply concerned with compulsions or a relationship with a substance, but a relationship with ultimate reality that quenches our thirst. The guys who started AA knew that the only way to combat the lesser spirits is with *the* Spirit, and that is just another way of saying we need to combat the counterfeit with reality.

Don't let the idea of being "spiritual" scare you off. True spirituality is simply desperation, and all humans are desperate to experience wholeness. We're all spiritual whether we are willing to admit it or not because we all want transcendence—something to elevate us beyond our limited, often painful experience. And when we don't find transcendence in dirt-under-our-fingernails reality, we look for it elsewhere. We give ourselves to the lesser spirits and our lives become unmanageable.

But when, in our desperation, we give ourselves to the Spirit who hovers over our dark emptiness, ultimate reality invades our lives and brings order from chaos.

Ultimate Reality

The radically good news is that transcendence is ours for the taking by faith. The tragically bad news is that we are broken people in a withered world at war with the very source of our healing. The problem at the root of all our problems has actually been solved, but we reject the solution at every turn.

We have unlimited access to the source of all life, goodness, and peace. God designed us in his image to live filled with himself—like plants filled with water— and his Spirit waits for us to drink him in. Yeah, things were a bit dicey there for a while. God's image walked out on him and we went to war against our heavenly Father. Living independently left us wilted and in need of transformation, but we've been reunited by God's grace.

In 2 Corinthians 5:19 we read, "God was in Christ reconciling the world to Himself, not imputing their trespasses to them." There is no greater reconciliation than God and man as one. Jesus is the reunion of creation with creator, and he said, "The one who comes to Me I will by no means cast out" (John 6:37). Anyone who wants in can be a part of his body—at peace with God and filled with his Spirit.

And what do we experience when Jesus receives us? Nothing short of union with the Trinity! Jesus told the Father, "The glory which You gave Me I have given them, that they may be one just as We are one: I in them, and You in Me; that they may be made perfect in one" (John 17:22–23). *This is the thirst-quenching living water of ultimate reality.* The wholeness we long for is ours if we would only believe it.

Many of us live like we're still at war with God, but the simple fact is the war is over. We can come home and it will be like we never left.

We can get on with living in union with God the way we were supposed to. Get that right and transformation is the natural consequence, just like parched plants stand up straight when they're watered. God fixed the mother of all problems, and he did it with no help from us. It really is finished. You'd think all of humanity would rejoice and run to him for healing, but we don't.

Why?

Because turning to God for help requires that we accept our helplessness. Rather than seeing his salvation as a peace offering, we see it as an assault on our pride. We desperately want to save ourselves, and that desire is at the heart of every addiction from booze to religion. That's why pagans and religious people alike both despise grace—God's free and unmerited acceptance. We have to open empty hands and accept grace from above.

In our self-imposed alienation from God, we think it's up to us to rise above our suffering or sin. We think we can control when and where we get relief from pain.

Running from Reality

Reality is overflowing with the Spirit, God's merciful presence, all of the undeserved blessings and joys in life, and on top of that, access to the Godhead and the ultimate redemption of the worst evil this bent world can dish out. But reality is also infected with the pain of what we've done, what we've left undone, and what's been done to us. Sobriety is letting all that hit you with full force.

Sharon Hersh, a therapist and an addiction expert, teaches that addicts believe two things that fuel their destructive behavior. The addict believes she deserves relief, and that she should be able to choose when and how she gets it. In that sense, we're all prone to addiction.

We all feel alone, aching for the wholeness that's ours if we would only believe it. We all try to ignore the reality of our pain and the healing presence of the Spirit. When we refuse to embrace the pain and pleasure of ultimate reality, what's left except to seek relief from the lesser spirits? We look for transcendence in the next bottle, the next achievement, the next sexual encounter, the next purchase, the next distraction, the next hit, or even the next commitment to holiness. We become addicted to seeking wholeness on our own terms.

However, when we turn to behaviors that seem to provide protection from pain, we build walls that cut us off from all we were created to enjoy. That's easy to see in the behavior of a raging drug addict, but it also happens when we try to control our world through religion and power, or simply seek relief in shopping, sex, food, achievement—pick your prison. Maintaining our walls takes more and more effort while giving less and less relief. We're all users and abusers, but addiction sets in when we abandon reality in exchange for self-protection. We can't selectively numb out; the ache and the ecstasy both go when we give up on reality. When we become addicted to providing our own relief, paradoxically, pleasure is drained from our lives as those lives prove to be unmanageable.

Living sober in union with the Spirit is the alternative. To do that, we have to be willing to let the waves of pain knock us down so the pleasure can wash over us. That's scary. We have to own all the ways we've hurt ourselves and others. We have to name all that we've lost, mourn, and ultimately accept that it's gone. We have to trust that because of Jesus, we really are one with God, give ourselves to the cycle of death and resurrection, let go and hope for redemption. We have to face the fear that relief may never come, and then choose to trust the Spirit. That's *so* scary that we don't want to even entertain that possibility—until avoiding our pain becomes more painful than the pain of changing.

Addiction gets us to that point.

It's so tempting to settle for comforting ourselves. But remember, true spirituality is simply desperation. Nobody is as spiritual as the addict who has encountered the futility of running from pain.

Paradoxically, that is the gift of addiction.

The Gift of Addiction

Sobriety is simply embracing reality, and nothing shoves reality in our faces like a full-blown addiction. Addiction gets worse the more we try to manage it. It gets stronger and ratchets up the pain until it's unavoidable.

Above all the lies we tell ourselves, addiction screams the truth: You are not in control!

Some fight the reality of their powerlessness until the day their addiction finally kills them, but not the addicts who accept they've hit rock bottom. The burned-out self-saviors get to realize the truth of humanity's helplessness before we die. That's a divine gift. Our broken lives are proof that we can't escape pain and we certainly can't fix ourselves.

Follow the trail of wreckage from all our futile efforts and it will lead to a loving God who offers what has always been ours—himself. He is the water that quenches the raging addict's thirst and the wholeness we looked for everywhere else when he was with us the entire time.

His Spirit and his Scriptures assure us that he is the only one truly in control, and that is not something to be feared or fought. In his sovereignty he promises to fill us with his life, to cause us to grow, and to work all things together for good. In other words, he will redeem our pain.

Yes, our addictions wreck us, but in God's hands, we're wrecked for life. The only way you will be able to see the raw beauty of that truth is to receive your help-lessness as a gift from God. Give up the idea that you are in control of when and where you get relief, or even victory over addiction, and he will use your compulsions to draw you to himself.

Trust Him

So, come. Come drunk, hungover, or high. Come angry. Come self-righteous. Come scared and ashamed. Come hurting. Come lonely. Jesus says, "Come to Me, all you who labor and are heavy laden, and I will give you rest" (Matthew 11:28).

Don't make any more promises you know you can't keep, just come. You won't have to go far because he's right there with you. All it takes is a nod in his direction or an open hand and the tears will flow out as his Spirit flows in.

You can stop trying to fix yourself because Jesus has given you the gift of his perfection to call your own. You can rest in his ever-present care. You can stop running from your pain and instead enter into it to find that pain is the place where you will encounter God in the most profound ways.

Come to him and transformation will begin to happen in his presence. All you have to do is trust him. Philippians 1:6 tells us, "He who has begun a good work in you will complete it until the day of Jesus Christ."

My mentor, Steve Brown, taught me something about that verse that has been a huge comfort and source of hope for me. It's essentially this: God finishes what he starts. If you've opened yourself to the presence of God, if God has done anything at all in your life, the very fact that there is a beginning is the promise of its completion.

> His divine power has given to us all things that pertain to life and godliness, through the knowledge of Him who called us by glory and virtue, by which have been given to us exceedingly great and precious promises, that through these you may be partakers of the divine nature . . . (2 Peter 1:3–4)

Transformation is simply a side benefit of walking in union with God. We will see that it happens slowly, little by little as you dare to accept the Spirit's invitation to trade the pain of not changing for the lesser pain of changing, but it will happen. God will redeem your pain. In the end, transformation, like helplessness and transcendence, is a gift, not an achievement.

You Are Safe

We're going to turn to some specific examples of what transformation in union with God looks like. However, before we look at how God redeems our pain, it's vitally important that you understand just how unbreakable your union with God is. Transformation is a messy business and you're going to need to remember in the dark what God showed you in the light.

First Corinthians 6:15 contains a hidden hope: "Do you not know that your bodies are members of Christ? Shall I then take the members of Christ and make them members of a harlot? Certainly not!"

Prior to that verse the apostle Paul told the Corinthians that all things were lawful, but not necessarily helpful. Then he brings up picking up a hooker. Certainly there are some negative consequences at this point, but those consequences do not include God leaving the believer. In fact, he says that believers are so "one" with Jesus, that if we have sex with a prostitute, Jesus is having sex with a prostitute. He goes on to remind believers that we are the temple of the Spirit.

Isn't that great news? The ultimate reality of your union with God can't be undone by your bad choices! Even if you're drunk or high right now, even if you just gave in to temptation or you're planning to give in, God is right there with you, loving you no matter what.

That will drive uptight religious people nuts, but if you're an addict who has tried to quit over and over and over again, that will give you hope in the midst of all the shame and guilt. "For I am persuaded that neither death nor life, nor angels nor principalities nor powers, nor things present nor things to come, nor height nor depth, nor any other created thing, shall be able to separate us from the love of God which is in Christ Jesus our Lord" (Romans 8:38–39).

Spiritus contra spiritum! Focus on the joy of your union with God instead of your addiction and the attraction to your addiction will fade. After all, it's your addiction that is making your life unmanageable.

Will you dare to believe that you already have the transcendence you're looking for in your lesser spirits? Will you dare to thank God even in the midst of your addiction? Will you dare to let him redeem your pain? If so, you may not stop acting on your compulsions right away, but you will begin to live sober . . . and you will always be as loved and as close to the Father as Jesus.

Redeeming the Pain

The problem at the root of all problems has been solved. Thirst-quenching, unbreakable union with our heavenly Father is ours through faith in Jesus's finished work. His Spirit within us is the clean, living water of ultimate reality bubbling up in the muck of day-to-day life. We can expect that our lives will be slowly transformed in the light of God's unconditional love and presence. His Spirit will wash away the lesser spirits to which we're addicted as we embrace the reality of inescapable pain—instead of running from suffering.

God will redeem our pain, but how does that play out practically? How do we move from accepting reality to thriving within it? In short, practice. We have to practice living sober.

Let's look at three practical ways we can practice living sober and trust the Spirit to use pain for good in our lives and in the lives we touch. They are compassion, creative expression, and connection.

Compassion

Practicing sobriety by embracing our pain helps us to receive compassion and makes us more compassionate toward others in pain. Suffering is a catalyst for compassion.

A few years ago I got really mad at my six-year-old son. He didn't actually do anything wrong, but what he did struck a raw nerve in me and I reacted. I had called him over to me and motioned for him to sit on my lap. I had been fighting with my wife, and I just wanted to sit in my son's presence. There's nothing like the wide-eyed adoration of your children to make you believe all the effort to raise them is worth it. But he wouldn't listen.

"Come sit with Daddy." I'm sure the tone in my voice the second time was more intense.

He climbed up into my lap, but his squirming made it clear he'd rather go back to whatever he was doing. I was being denied the comfort and validation I sought. He elbowed me, and I pushed him off my lap.

"Fine, go!" I yelled. Anger over my son's perceived rejection was instantly mixed with shame over my reaction.

Later that week I recounted the event to my therapist. We talked about my memories from when I was six years old. One in particular became the focus of our conversation.

Thirty-five years ago, I lay on my bed beating my head with a toy baseball bat.

"What were you feeling?" my counselor asked. I searched in the darkness for an answer, but nothing came to mind except, "I want to be alone, but I don't want to be alone, and I don't know what that means."

I kept repeating it to the counselor over and over again: "I want to be alone, but I don't want to be alone, and I don't know what that means." My head swelled with the words, and I just wanted the confusing thoughts to stop. My counselor watched as I started to beat on my forehead with my fist. "I want to be alone, but I don't want to be alone, and I don't know what that means." No matter how hard I hit myself, I couldn't get the words out of my head.

I left counseling that day bruised and exhausted. I didn't have any answers as to what was going on with me as a kid. But I knew in my gut that it hurt bad to be six years old because I had just relived it. I had entered into long-ignored, festering pain.

I thought of my six-year-old son. I imagined him in bed beating his head with a bat. It made me sick to my stomach. I just wanted to let him know that I understood how hard it was to be such a helpless little guy in such a big confusing world. *If an earthly father can get that, how much more our Father in heaven?* As Carl Jung once wrote,

> The acceptance of oneself is the essence of the whole moral problem and the epitome of a whole outlook on life. That I feed the hungry, that I forgive an insult, that I love my enemy in the name of Christ—all these are undoubtedly great virtues. What I do unto the least of my brethren, that I do unto Christ. But what if I should discover that the least among them all, the poorest of all the beggars, the most impudent of all the offenders, the very enemy himself—that these are within me, and that I myself stand in need of the alms of my

own kindness—that I myself am the enemy who must be loved—what then? As a rule, the Christian's attitude is then reversed; there is no longer any question of love or long-suffering; we say to the brother within us "Raca," and condemn and rage against ourselves. We hide it from the world; we refuse to admit ever having met this least among the lowly in ourselves.[2]

I am the selfish enemy who didn't get the adoration he wanted from his young son so he turned on him. But why? Because the enemy inside me is actually a neglected child who is so insecure he wouldn't know what to do with attention if he received it. "I want to be alone, but I don't want to be alone . . ." and until this moment, writing this, I didn't know what that means.

Our suffering and sin are tied together, but when you see only the sin, you tend to see a monster rather than a person. It's only when you see the whole person—their pain, their fear, their desire, their suffering, and their sin—that you can begin to understand the compassion of Jesus. Jesus looked with compassion on lost, confused, demanding crowds who wouldn't give him a moment's peace because he saw them as vulnerable sheep without a shepherd to guide and protect them. Jesus asked that his tormentors and murderers be forgiven because they couldn't possibly understand the horror of their actions. Jesus's compassion comes to us in our weakest, most sinful moments.

Yes, I am my own worst enemy, but Jesus teaches us to love our enemies.

That night I tucked my son in and lay next to him. I cried and told him I was sorry for pushing him away. He forgave me, and the compassion of the Spirit filled the room. Until I embraced the hurting child within myself, I had less compassion for my boy. That may sound strange, but it's impossible to deny part of yourself and be a whole person. I couldn't love my son well and keep beating my own head.

I had to start by looking at the reality of my life. My compassion for my son depended on me embracing my pain and receiving compassion from God. What's more, my apology to my son opened the door to the experience of the Spirit's compassion through him. I received absolution from my son as he incarnated unconditional love.

By embracing a hard reality, I moved deeper into sobriety. I touched the healing transcendent in daily life. I didn't need a drink to comfort me because my pain was redeemed.

Creative Expression

Welcoming the reality of our pain can also give birth to the creative expression of the Spirit.

Julie Burstein is a fellow radio producer who has spent her career interviewing a lot of very creative people. She's also the author of *Spark: How Creativity Works*. One of the most important things Julie has learned about creativity is this:

> For creativity to flourish [requires] the embrace of loss, the oldest and most constant of human experiences . . . The story that we all live [is] the cycle of creation and destruction,

of control and letting go, of picking up the pieces and making something new.[3]

The best artists expose the festering boil of their lives, and then, with the skill of a surgeon, they cut it open and express the infection for the world to see. When that happens, we stand in awe of their honesty and bravery. Our unexpressed pain aches with the truth of the human experience we're witnessing. If only for an evening, or a moment, we know that we are not alone in our suffering—and that makes all the difference.

Life is brutal. Nobody makes it out unscathed. Everybody gets hurt. Everyone has scars. It's how you deal with pain in life that matters. The artist creates something beautiful from brutality, thereby redeeming the pain. The Spirit is the ultimate artist, picking up the broken pieces of our lives and making something new. Sobriety is living open to the creative expression of the divine in our lives.

What have you lost? Your childhood? Your innocence? Your health? A relationship with your father or mother? Your faith? A child?

It can all be put to music or painted on a canvas or written in a poem. The call to sobriety is the call to accept the reality that what you lost is gone, never to return as it once was, and to express the pain of that loss to the Spirit. Wail, yell, and scream. Let it all out and then listen.

In the silence you will hear a still small voice say, "You are not alone. Look at the Incarnation. See how I didn't leave humanity alone in its suffering? I chose to suffer as you do. I was betrayed and murdered. A Father lost his Son that day. But it didn't end there. I redeemed the pain and brought life from death, the breath of the Spirit and resurrection to all who believe."

While all that we lost will never return as it was, the loss can be redeemed. I know it hurts, but God delights in working all things together for good. Jesus endured the cross for the joy set before him. He did it to see the tears running down your smiling face when you finally encounter the staggering beauty of what he made out of your mess.

When we invite that creative expression of the Spirit in and through our lives, it frees us to give voice to our pain, thereby encouraging others. It's very much like becoming more compassionate by receiving compassion. As you get honest about your suffering, over and over again, you will hear people say, "You too?" The Spirit will whisper to them through your incarnation, "You are not alone."

As comedian Jon Stewart put it, "We've come from the same history—2,000 years of persecution—we've just expressed our sufferings differently as people. Blacks developed the blues. Jews complained, we just never thought of putting it to music."[4] You can either complain or create. You're going to suffer. Why waste it? Start singing the blues. You might even end up in joyous worship.

Connection

Finally, facing our pain can also lead to deeper human connection. As we live in union with God, he will redeem our pain to strengthen the relationships that enrich our lives.

Connection with others actually helps us overcome our addictions. That's plain to see in the success of 12-step groups, and I know from personal experience that I'm more prone to turn to alcohol, porn, or drugs when I'm looking for relief from the loneliness of my self-imposed isolation from friends and family.

In addition, new research also suggests the importance of human connection in overcoming addictions. You can read about some of these studies in Johann Hari's book *Chasing the Scream: The First and Last Days of the War on Drugs*. Hari quoted a professor in the Netherlands named Peter Choen and said:

> . . . maybe we shouldn't even call it addiction. Maybe we should call it bonding. Human beings have a natural and innate need to bond, and when we're happy and healthy, we'll bond and connect with each other, but if you can't do that, because you're traumatized or isolated or beaten down by life, you will bond with something that will give you some sense of relief. Now, that might be gambling, that might be pornography, that might be cocaine, that might be cannabis, but you will bond and connect with something because that's our nature. That's what we want as human beings.[5]

We were created for communion with God, but we were also created for communion with one another.

In fact, since people are the image of God, we love him when we love one another. That's practical. Jesus said,

> "'You shall love the LORD your God with all your heart, with all your soul, and with all your mind.' This is the first and great commandment. And the second is like it: 'You shall love your neighbor as yourself.' On these two commandments hang all the Law and the Prophets." (Matthew 22:37–40)

The second commandment is like the first because we accomplish the first by doing the second. We love God by loving his image.

> If someone says, "I love God," and hates his brother, he is a liar; for he who does not love his brother [made in God's image] whom he has seen, how can he love God whom he has not seen? (1 John 4:20)

There's a mysterious interaction with God when we love one another, and that love is deeply satisfying. So much so that our love affair with our lesser spirits becomes less attractive when we have real, loving relationships.

That all sounds great on paper, but we have decided to face reality, and the reality is that love hurts. There's no escape. It's a fact you have to deal with if you're going to enjoy intimate relationships. In John 15:13 we read that Jesus said, "Greater love has no one than this, than to lay down one's life for his friends."

So there you have it. The object of your love will kill you. Love is suffering and ultimately death for the beloved, and we all love someone or something. Many addicts lay their lives down for love of their addictions, but there's another option. If we're going to suffer anyway, why not choose to suffer to incarnate love the way Jesus did? Why not redeem the pain of difficult relationships so we can enjoy the connection with loved ones we long for?

As Steve Brown says, "You can't love until you've been loved, and then you can only love to the degree to which you have been loved." Look at all the damage you've done. Start there. Own it. But don't stop there. Receive the unconditional love of God. Jesus paid the price for our sins when he laid down his life for us on the cross. When you accept how much you've been forgiven and how much that cost, you can forgive others instead of making them pay for their sins against you.

When we forgive like we've been forgiven, our relationships deepen. We can have mercy when others act out of their pain because we know what it's like to hurt. We can even share pain with one another, and that is one of the most intimate things people do.

The only way to have deep relationships is to accept the pain that comes with them. If we do, we will experience the power that human connection has to help free us from our addictions.

Time to Sober Up

Jesus said, "In the world you will have tribulation; but be of good cheer, I have overcome the world"

(John 16:33). Jesus overcame the world through his life, death, and resurrection, and he's slowly, almost imperceptibly, redeeming everything—you, me, our pain, and all of creation. For the joy of that redemption set before him, he entered into the suffering of the cross (Hebrews 12:2). When we embrace our pain like Jesus did with his cross, we join him in working all things together for good. He makes us more compassionate, creative, and connected.

As fallen creatures without the Spirit, we are weak, needy, and susceptible to all sorts of addictions. But as creatures in communion with our Creator, we have embraced reality by faith. We are sober. We are the image of God, filled with his Spirit, and by his strength in our weakness we can enjoy making good choices. It's been proven over and over again. Yes, sometimes as children of God we choose to disobey our loving Father who wants the best for us. But we never stop being his children, and that is sobering. Our lives will never be without sin or struggles, but by God's grace, living in union with the Spirit, our lives can become quite manageable.

> Beloved, now we are children of God; and it has not yet been revealed what we shall be, but we know that when He is revealed, we shall be like Him, for we shall see Him as He is. (1 John 3:2)

That's our ultimate reality, but never forget—the only people who get better are people who know that if they never get better, God will love them anyway.

Endnotes

1. C. G. Jung, Gerhard Adler, and Aniela Jaffé, *Selected Letters of C. G. Jung, 1909–1961* (Princeton: Princeton University Press, 1984), 198.

2. Carl G. Jung, "Psychotherapists or the Clergy," *Modern Man in Search of a Soul* (London: Routledge, 2001), 240–41.

3. TED: Ideas worth spreading "Julie Burstein: 4 Lessons in Creativity" TED Talk video/transcript, 17:20. February 2012. http://www.ted.com/talks/julie_burstein_4_lessons_in_creativity.

4. Jon Stewart, "One Night Only: An All-Star Comedy Tribute to Don Rickles," YouTube video, 1:22:48, May 28, 2014. https://www.youtube.com/watch?v=T2rUH1xRTdE.

5. TED: Ideas worth spreading "Johann Hari: Everything you think you know about addiction is wrong" TED Talk video/transcript, 14:42. June 2015. http://www.ted.com/talks/johann_hari_everything_you_think_you_know_about_addiction_is_wrong.